Endorsements for the Church Questions Series

"Christians are pressed by very real questions. How does Scripture structure a church, order worship, organize ministry, and define biblical leadership? Those are just examples of the questions that are answered clearly, carefully, and winsomely in this new series from 9Marks. I am so thankful for this ministry and for its incredibly healthy and hopeful influence in so many faithful churches. I eagerly commend this series."

R. Albert Mohler Jr., President, The Southern Baptist Theological Seminary

"Sincere questions deserve thoughtful answers. If you're not sure where to start in answering these questions, let this series serve as a diving board into the pool. These minibooks are winsomely to-the-point and great to read together with one friend or one hundred friends."

Gloria Furman, author, *Missional Motherhood* and *The Pastor's Wife*

"As a pastor, I get asked lots of questions. I'm approached by unbelievers seeking to understand the gospel, new believers unsure about next steps, and maturing believers wanting help answering questions from their Christian family, friends, neighbors, or coworkers. It's in these moments that I wish I had a book to give them that was brief, answered their questions, and pointed them in the right direction for further study. Church Questions is a series that provides just that. Each booklet tackles one question in a biblical, brief, and practical manner. The series may be called Church Questions, but it could be called 'Church Answers.' I intend to pick these up by the dozens and give them away regularly. You should too."

Juan R. Sanchez, Senior Pastor, High Pointe Baptist Church, Austin, Texas

"Where can we Christians find reliable answers to our common questions about life together at church—without having to plow through long, expensive books? The Church Questions booklets meet our need with answers that are biblical, thoughtful, and practical. For pastors, this series will prove a trustworthy resource for guiding church members toward deeper wisdom and stronger unity."

Ray Ortlund, President, Renewal Ministries

Does the Gospel Promise Health and Prosperity?

Church Questions

Does the Gospel Promise Health and Prosperity?

Sean DeMars

CROSSWAY

WHEATON, ILLINOIS

Trade paperback ISBN: 978-1-4335-7851-9
ePub ISBN: 978-1-4335-7854-0
PDF ISBN: 978-1-4335-7852-6
Mobipocket ISBN: 978-1-4335-7853-3

Library of Congress Cataloging-in-Publication Data

Names: DeMars, Sean, 1986- author.
Title: Does the gospel promise health and prosperity? / Sean DeMars.
Description: Wheaton, Illinois : Crossway, 2022. | Series: Church questions | Includes bibliographical references and index.
Identifiers: LCCN 2021027433 (print) | LCCN 2021027434 (ebook) | ISBN 9781433578540 (trade paperback) | ISBN 9781433578526 (pdf) | ISBN 9781433578533 (mobipocket) | ISBN 9781433578540 (ebk)
Subjects: LCSH: Faith movement (Hagin) | Wealth--Religious aspects--Christianity. | Health--Religious aspects--Christianity.
Classification: LCC BR1643.5 .D46 2022 (print) | LCC BR1643.5 (ebook) | DDC 289.9/4--dc23
LC record available at https://lccn.loc.gov/2021027433
LC ebook record available at https://lccn.loc.gov/2021027434

Crossway is a publishing ministry of Good News Publishers.

BP		31	30	29	28	27	26	25	24	23	22
15	14	13	12	11	10	9	8	7	6	5	4	3	2	1

For it has been granted to you that for the
sake of Christ you should not only believe
in him but also suffer for his sake.

Philippians 1:29

I was sitting in my bathtub, unable to get up. I felt like I was about to die. The water in the tub had grown cold. I'd been marinating in my own soup stock for two hours. I'd been drifting in and out of consciousness. Whenever I was coherent enough to pray, I did. I prayed for healing, and I prayed for the faith to receive my healing.

> *Jesus, please, save me. Please, heal me. I repent, I put my whole heart into prayer right now, and I cast out any doubt or fear. I know you can heal me. Please heal me!*

Finally, my mother pulled me out of the bathtub. "Look at you!" she said through tears. "I'm taking you to the ER—now!"

I could barely speak. "No! Jesus is my doctor."

In my mind, this is what it looked like to follow Christ.

I'd only been a Christian for a few months. I was fresh out of jail, and most of my days were spent trying to share the gospel with people that I used to do drugs with or sell drugs to. During these early days, I met a man named Roger, who—unlike anyone else in the neighborhood—invited me into his home for a meal. Roger bought me lunch and spent all day teaching me about the Bible.[1]

Over the next six months, Roger fed me, counseled me, helped me out financially, and taught me how to read my Bible. Unfortunately, what he taught me was wrong. Like, really wrong. He taught me something called "the prosperity gospel." I'm fairly confident that no Christian knew less about Scripture than I did, so I had no idea that the theological Kool-Aid Roger was serving me was laced with arsenic.

And I drank it all.

Roger's teaching made sense at the time. "Look, she touched the hem of his garment and was healed. . . . Look, Jesus couldn't heal them because they didn't have enough faith." The prosperity gospel seemed self-evidently true from Scripture. It was so plain, even obvious.

But things weren't panning out in real life. I couldn't pay my rent. I struggled to make ends meet every week. I was getting sick even when I claimed healing in Jesus's name. Where was the victory? The prosperity gospel math wasn't adding up.

"Hey Roger," I said. "I don't understand. It seems like this stuff isn't working. What am I doing wrong? What am I missing?"

"I don't know exactly what it is, Sean, but I know the problem ain't with God or his word. It's got to be something in your heart or in your life."

During those early days as a Christian, I genuinely loved Jesus. He saved me, and I wanted to spend the rest of my life serving him. In my mind, rebuking illness, claiming prosperity, and searching the deep, dark recesses of my heart for sin and doubt was what I thought Jesus wanted from me. I didn't know any better, so I did what I knew.

Then one day, God intervened. A true Bible teacher showed me what the gospel was *really* all about.

I don't remember many of the details of that night, but when I heard someone genuinely preach the biblical gospel, I realized that most of what I thought I knew about God, the Bible, the cross, and the Christian life was wrong. Dead wrong. Those were dark days. I was full of anger, confusion, and depression. But God reshaped my understanding of the gospel with a right understanding of his word.[2]

Today, I serve as a pastor of a church in North Alabama. It's been a long time since I believed in the prosperity gospel, but I continue to see its damaging effect on the church that Jesus purchased with his own blood. I'm writing this booklet to help you think rightly about the prosperity gospel for the sake of your own soul (2 John 2:8) and to equip you for the work of evangelism and discipling.

I plan to stick to the big questions about the prosperity gospel. Questions like:

- What is the prosperity gospel?
- Is the prosperity gospel biblical?
- How can we help others who might believe in the prosperity gospel?

What Is "The Prosperity Gospel"?

When I talk to my English-speaking friends overseas, I'm reminded of the old quip that Americans, Brits, and Aussies are separated by a common language. The English say "boot" and I (an American) think of what cowboys have on their feet. But they're referring to their vehicle's trunk space. My Australian friends use the word "diary" to refer to their schedule, not the books that teenage girls keep hidden under their pillows. Brits, Aussies, and North Americans all speak English, but sometimes we use the same words to communicate different things.

This can happen when we talk about theology. So I want to make sure that before we start talking about "the prosperity gospel," we understand the words we're using and how we're using them. We need to define our terms.

But before we get to those definitions, let's talk about one of my favorite subjects: food. Because if you're going to understand the prosperity gospel you need to understand Mexican food.

I'm something of a Mexican food aficionado. I grew up in southern California, so my love runs deep. Whenever I travel, I usually try to find a local Mexican food spot to try their version of a taco. I've tried Korean tacos, Tex-Mex tacos, vegan tacos, and every iteration in-between. But here's the thing about Mexican food. Whatever you're having, it's usually just a variation of the same ingredients: meat, cheese, tortillas, vegetables, and some kind of salsa. Mexican food may look one way in southern California, another way in Mexico City, and still another way in south Boston, but wherever you have these ingredients, there you have Mexican food.

That's a pretty good picture of what the prosperity gospel is like. The prosperity gospel isn't a single idea or doctrine. It's a collection of ideas which, when taken together confuse, distort, and undermine the true gospel of Jesus Christ. It may look one way in South America, another way in India, and still another way in the suburbs of North Georgia. But wherever you go, the prosperity gospel usually has the same basic ingredients. So rather than offering a one-sentence definition of "the prosperity gospel," I'm going to lay out four of its core ingredients.

1. God wants to give us material prosperity.
2. God wants us to speak with power.
3. God doesn't want us to suffer.
4. God wants us to live the victorious, prosperous life.

I'll explain them each in turn.

1. God Wants to Give Us Material Prosperity

The prosperity gospel emphasizes that God wants to bless his people with material goods. How God does this will depend on the context. Prosperity preachers in suburban Texas will likely tell you that God wants you to drive cars with leather seats and have a bustling 401(k). Prosperity preachers in rural Africa might suggest that God wants his people to have chickens that lay eggs and bumper crops every season. Whatever the context, every form of the prosperity gospel suggests that our relationship with God through Christ should yield material goods in our lives.

> *The problem with this way of thinking is that it values God's blessings more than God himself. It teaches people to love the gifts above the giver.*

Certainly, God delights to give good gifts to his people (Matt. 7:7–11). But these heavenly gifts are ultimately supposed to point us back to God himself. As Paul said, "[God] gives to all mankind life and breath and everything . . . that they should seek God, and perhaps feel their way toward him and find him" (Acts 17:25, 27).

Do you see that? God gives us good things in order to point us back to him.

And yet, the prosperity gospel subtly, perhaps even unintentionally, teaches people to think about God as a means of getting what we want. It doesn't teach people to want God for himself. In the prosperity gospel, the good news of the gospel is financial success, personal wellness, healing from sickness, or accruing any number of other gifts from God.

Simply put, this is idolatry. It construes God as a genie more than a heavenly Father. Compare what you've just read to Asaph's words in Psalm 73:

> Whom have I in heaven but you?
>> And there is nothing on earth that
>>> I desire besides you.
> My flesh and my heart may fail,
>> but God is the strength of my heart
>>> and my portion forever.
>>> (Ps. 73:25–26)

Does it sound like Asaph cares more about God's gifts or God himself? In Scripture, God is the highest end, the greatest gift.

2. God Wants Us to Speak with Power

The prosperity gospel teaches that when we come to Christ our words can tap into God's creative power. Through Jesus Christ, prosperity gospel preachers claim, we can speak reality into existence. Sometimes this is called "name it and claim it"—we "name" a blessing and then "claim" it as our own, expecting that it will become a reality.

> *The problem with this way of thinking is that it confuses two essential, unflinching truths from Scripture: God is the Creator, and we are his creatures.*

Let me explain.

First, the prosperity gospel remakes God in our image. Scripture teaches that God created humans in the image and likeness of God (Gen. 1:27). The prosperity gospel, however, inverts this truth and refashions God in our own image such that our interests and ambitions necessarily become his.

Of course, the prosperity gospel isn't the only false religion to refashion God according to our own tastes. Sinful humans have been doing that for millennia. Consider the gods of the Greco-Roman pantheon. Ares and Artemis, Zeus and Demetir, each of these "gods" are unmistakably human. They're often petty—just like us; they're full of malice, lust, and greed— just like us. What we see in these "gods" is not true divinity but merely a reflection of our own fallen image.

This may look different on TBN—a television network that openly promotes the prosperity gospel—than it looked in the ancient Roman Pantheon. But the careful observer will recognize the same phenomenon. The prosperity gospel conforms God's desires to line up with ours, rather than conforming our desires to his.

Put simply, the prosperity gospel is a religion of greed (1 Thess. 2:5). It trains Christians to view Jesus as a God who primarily wants us to be abundantly prosperous in every way, who never decrees our sickness or our suffering, and whose sole concern is his creatures' comfort.

When God created us in his image, he sat back and called his work "good" (Gen. 1:27, 31). But when Adam and Eve sinned, they marred his good and beautiful creation. When we try to sinfully recreate God in our image, we distort his identity and disfigure his character. The prosperity gospel paints a picture of Jesus that makes him look more like the petty gods of ancient Greece and Rome than the eternal Son of God.

Second, the prosperity gospel teaches us to speak things into existence—something only God can do. In the beginning, God spoke, and stuff happened (Genesis 1). The universe came into existence. Why? Because God speaks things into existence. Human beings can't do this because human beings aren't God. But according to many prosperity gospel teachers, all Christians have the ability to speak things into existence, blessings and curses alike. As strange as it may seem, this false teaching flows almost entirely out of a misunderstanding of just one verse, Proverbs 18:21.

> Death and life are in the power of the
> tongue,
>   and those who love it will eat its
>   fruits.

Prosperity gospel teachers suggest that this verse indicates that if we want something, then we simply need to "name it and claim it." We simply need to speak it into existence.

The problem, of course, is that Proverbs 18:21 doesn't mean that at all.

Let's have a quick lesson on how to interpret proverbs in the Bible. Proverbs are maxims, pithy nuggets of wisdom about how to live life to the glory of God in a fallen world. They provide insight on how to live with the grain of God's created order. So the point of this proverb is not "humans have the power to create prosperity with their words." The point of this proverb is that what we choose to do with our words will either communicate grace and encouragement (i.e., "life") or discouragement and despair (i.e., "death").

James, likely relying on Proverbs, teaches this same idea when he compares our tongues to small fires that can set a forest ablaze (James 3:5). When we curse others, James says, our tongue is "a restless evil, full of deadly poison" (James 3:8). Obviously, he's speaking metaphorically. Our tongues aren't literally poisonous just as they don't literally create life or cause death. These descriptions simply symbolize the power of our words to build up or tear down.

Furthermore, to suggest that we can speak material blessings into existence contradicts the rest of Scripture. The Bible regularly and consistently teaches that God *alone* has the power to speak life into existence by the power of his word (Rom. 4:17).

Prosperity gospel teachers disagree. They say that when we become Christians, we tap into the same creative power that God alone has. But Scripture rejects those claims as not only dangerous, but damning. Remember, Satan tries to lead people astray by telling them they can be like God (Gen. 3:5). Anyone who tells you that you can be like God and speak material blessings into existence is following in the footsteps of the deceiver.

3. God Doesn't Want Us to Suffer

The prosperity gospel suggests that because God is our Father he would never want his children to suffer. In fact, if a Christian is suffering, it's likely because of sin or at least a lack of faith. Truly faith-filled Christians will know physical health and wholeness.

> *The problem with this way of thinking is that God promises his people that they will suffer in this world.*

Sometimes we suffer because of sin—either our own sin or the sins of others (e.g., 2 Sam. 12:19, Ps. 32:3–4). But Scripture also teaches us that people suffer because of God's good but strange providence.

God often uses our suffering to accomplish something beautiful and good in the lives of his children (Gen. 50:20; Job 1; John 9:1–3; 2 Cor. 12:7–10). This point is certainly true of the sufferings of the perfectly innocent and faithful Lord Jesus, which were clearly the will of God (Isa. 53:10; Acts 4:27–28).

Many New Testament authors teach that suffering is a normal part of the Christian's experience. Look at how God speaks to his people about their troubles:

> Blessed are you when others revile you and persecute you and utter all kinds of evil against you falsely on my account. Rejoice and be glad, for your reward is great in heaven, for so they persecuted the prophets who were before you. (Matt. 5:11–12)

> For it has been granted to you that for the sake of Christ you should not only believe in him but also suffer for his sake. (Phil. 1:29)

> Yet if anyone suffers as a Christian, let him not be ashamed, but let him glorify God in that name. (1 Pet. 4:16)

Despite these clear passages of Scripture, prosperity gospel teachers make Christians feel ashamed when they suffer. They tell people that God *always* wants to heal their diseases, which makes it really weird that a remarkably high percentage of humanity eventually dies. They tell people that God doesn't want them to suffer. But the Bible's teaching is much more complex. The Bible explains that sometimes God shows his love and power by healing and sparing us from suffering, and sometimes he uses pain and difficulty to bring himself glory as he sanctifies and ultimately saves his people.

4. God Wants Us to Live the Victorious, Prosperous Life

During my time in the prosperity gospel, I mainly heard sermons about four topics:

1. faith
2. wealth
3. health
4. victory

These four themes are the tracks that the prosperity preaching train run on. Why? Because prosperity and victory are the primary features of the Christian life.

The problem with this way of thinking is that Scripture teaches that the faithful Christian life can't be reduced to four or five themes.

In the course of my regular preaching ministry, my congregation has heard sermons on subjects such as grace, faith, humility, authority, the family, marriage, predestination, singing, suffering, obedience, blessings, adoption, pastoring, membership, hell, sanctification, election, discipleship, racial reconciliation, joy, the tabernacle, the sacrificial system, holiness, spiritual warfare, and more.

Our people have heard sermons on such a variety of subjects because our church is committed to expository preaching. I preach consecutively, verse-by-verse, through books of the Bible. In other words, God sets the agenda for what our church hears. We aim to live according to all that God has said, and we submit to the whole counsel of God.

On the other hand, prosperity gospel preachers pick and choose out-of-context verses to buttress their bad theology. In doing so, they also conveniently avoid any passages that contradict their message.

So, let me ask you: Are you being taught the whole counsel of God, verse-by-verse, in every book of the Bible? Are preachers consistently connecting those passage to the person and work of Jesus Christ, explaining who he is and how what he's done demands a response? Or do your preachers focus on the same four or five topics: favor, blessing, health, wealth, prosperity? If you hear messages on the same topics that *aren't* the gospel, then go somewhere else. Find a church that preaches the whole counsel of God. God's word is a banquet of truth; don't settle for a few crumbs.

Same Bible, Different Doctrine?

Now that we have a sense of the core elements of the prosperity gospel, let's dig a little deeper.

Those who believe in the prosperity gospel read the same Bible I do. So how is it possible that we come to wildly different conclusions?

Well, the answer lies in how we *interpret* Scripture. The prosperity gospel trained me to read Scripture in such a way that I saw all suffering as evidence of some spiritual shortcoming. I thought going to the doctor was a sin. I thought admitting I had a common cold proved my unbelief. I thought that saying the right things in the right way would unlock God's blessings for my life. Thankfully, I learned a better way to read, understand, and apply the truths of Scripture.

We would be wise to remember that not everyone who claims to be a teacher of God's word speaks God's truth. Remember, even Satan quoted Scripture to Jesus, and Jesus had to respond to Satan's distortions with a right understanding of God's word (Matt. 4:5–7). In fact, the Bible anticipates that false teachers will seek to deceive us by twisting the Scriptures (Acts 20:30; 2 Pet. 3:16).

There are a number of ways in which the prosperity gospel twists Scripture. Let's look at three.

First, the prosperity gospel teaches us to read the Bible through a man-centered lens, not a Christ-centered lens. Jesus taught that God's word is ultimately about him (Luke 24:13–35). God creates for his glory, he acts for his glory, and he saves sinners for his glory. In the Bible, God's glory is the beating heart of every passage. We, however, tend to think that the world revolves around us, and we read the Bible accordingly.

Even though we're all prone to misread Scripture in this self-centered way, most of us recognize it as a problem. But the prosperity gospel trains people to read Scripture this way. When I believed the prosperity gospel, I was taught to read Scripture by focusing on myself and on my personal experiences. I'd approach every text with the following questions:

- What does this text teach me about being blessed?
- What does this verse say about victory?
- How will this word lead me into greater financial prosperity?

In contrast to this me-centered way of reading the Bible, God wants us to read Scripture focusing on his works. As Paul writes, all things are "from him and through him and to him" (Rom. 11:36). Our Scripture reading should focus on God's acts of salvation, not on how to gain personal wealth.

Second, the prosperity gospel trains us to interpret texts out of context. As a young Christian, I wanted to keep the truth of God's word ever before my eyes. I would write Scripture on little scraps of paper and place them all over my house—on the bathroom mirror, on the fridge, on my alarm clock, anywhere my eyes would be drawn throughout the day. My bathroom-mirror Scripture was Romans 8:37: "We are more than conquerors."

The Scripture I saw every morning on my way out the door was Matthew 4:9: "All these things I will give you, if you will fall down and worship me." I took this verse as a promise: if I would serve the Lord faithfully, he would bless me abundantly and give me all the things of the world. As I stepped into a dark and broken world, I wanted this promise to strengthen my faith and commitment to the Lord.

But there's a problem. Matthew 4:9 isn't a promise from God. It's a temptation from Satan. Here's the verse in context:

Again, the devil took him to a very high mountain and showed him all the kingdoms of the world and their glory. And he said to him, "*All these I will give you, if you will fall down and worship me.*" Then Jesus said to him, "Be gone, Satan! For it is written,

"'You shall worship the Lord your God
And him only shall you serve.'"

Then the devil left him, and behold, angels came and were ministering to him. (Matt. 4:8–11)

Of course, I would have *known* Matthew 4:9 wasn't a promise if I had learned how to read Scripture in context, but the prosperity gospel depends on cherry-picking phrases without paying attention to the larger biblical narrative.

Reading verses out of context isn't unique to the prosperity gospel. None of us read God's word perfectly. We all approach it with less care than it deserves. But this way of reading the Bible *characterizes* the prosperity gospel; it's essential to it. It's also why prosperity preachers deceive so many professing Christians, many of whom genuinely desire to know and obey God's word but have never learned how to read it in context.

Third, the prosperity gospel fails to teach the big story of the Bible. The Bible unfolds the story of redemption. At the beginning of the story, man exists with God in perfect peace, harmony, and prosperity. But when sin enters into the world, death comes with it. Creation enters into a state of decay, and suffering becomes a normal part of the human experience (Gen. 3:17–19; Rom. 8:20).

But the story doesn't end there. In God's good timing, Jesus comes to make all things new by destroying sin and death on the cross and restoring all of the blessings of God's good creation through his resurrection (1 Cor. 15:54–57; Heb. 2:14). Although Jesus has already begun to make all things new, he will wait until the final chapter to bring this work to its culmination. The gospel promises us that all those who are found in Christ will live happily ever after (Isa. 65:17–25; Rev. 21:1–4, 22–27).

One of the main problems with the prosperity gospel is that it teaches Christians to believe that biblical promises are fulfilled here and now, when God himself only applies the same promises to the new heavens and new earth.

Consider, for example, God's promise for physical healing. The Bible promises every genuine Christian final, physical healing in the form of a glorified, resurrected body (1 Cor. 15:51–53). But many proponents of the prosperity gospel suggest that we can access the fullness of physical healing here and now, on this side of heaven. They say Jesus purchased our physical healing on the cross; *therefore*, every blood-bought believer can access the blessing of physical health *now*.

These assertions greatly misunderstand how the Bible's drama of redemption unfolds. Yes, Christ did ultimately purchase complete physical healing for his people. But those benefits are applied to Christ's people when our bodies are resurrected from the dead, when God fully and finally fulfills all his promises to the saints.

Teaching people that God promises to heal them here and now if they have enough faith is not only spiritually dangerous—it's deadly. Remember my story at the beginning? Thousands of prosperity gospel adherents testify to similar experiences, refusing medical help for serious issues because they just knew God would heal them—until he didn't. Advocates of the prosperity gospel harm their followers by offering them a hope that Jesus never promised.

How to Help Those Who Believe the Prosperity Gospel

So how do we help our family members, friends, coworkers, or even fellow church members who are swept up in the prosperity gospel? Here are a few simple ideas as you prayerfully engage their error.

Explain the True Gospel

The most important way to help is to teach them a right understanding of the gospel.

According to Scripture, the gospel says we were dead in sin (Eph. 2:1), separated from God, and destined for his holy wrath (Isa. 59:2). But even when we were dead in our sins, God loved us and sent his Son to die for us (Rom. 5:8). Through Jesus's death and resurrection, God has reconciled us to himself (2 Cor. 5:18). The benefits of Christ's work are applied to us personally when we recognize this message to be true and respond by repenting of our sin and trusting in Christ alone, joyfully recognizing Jesus's lordship over our lives (Mark 1:15; Rom. 10:9; 1 John 5:3). This free offer of salvation comes to us by God's grace alone, and we receive this salvation by faith alone (Rom. 4:5), a faith that is itself a gift from God (Eph. 2:8–9).

Let me suggest that as you explain the gospel, a good place to begin would be Isaiah 53—ironically, a passage prosperity preachers often use to defend their theology.

But he was pierced for our transgressions;
>   he was crushed for our iniquities;
> upon him was the chastisement that
> >   brought us peace,
> >   and with his wounds we are healed.
> >   (Isa. 53:5)

Prosperity preachers point to this verse as a promise of physical healing purchased by Jesus through his work on the cross. At first glance, that idea doesn't seem unreasonable. But is that really what the passage is saying?

When we're interpreting the Bible, one important rule to remember is that we must always let Scripture interpret Scripture. Furthermore, we always want to look to the New Testament anytime we're interpreting the Old Testament. After all, we want to interpret the Bible like Jesus and the apostles, right?

It turns out, the apostle Peter comments on Isaiah 53:5 in 1 Peter 2:21–25. Here's that passage in context:

> For to this you have been called, because Christ also suffered for you, leaving you an

example, so that you might follow in his steps. He committed no sin, neither was deceit found in his mouth. When he was reviled, he did not revile in return; when he suffered, he did not threaten, but continued entrusting himself to him who judges justly. *He himself bore our sins in his body on the tree, that we might die to sin and live to righteousness. By his wounds you have been healed.* For you were straying like sheep, but have now returned to the Shepherd and Overseer of your souls.

As you can see, Peter teaches that the prophet Isaiah wasn't promising that Jesus would bring *physical* healing, but *spiritual* healing—healing from our sin-sickness. Here it is again:

He himself bore our sins in his body on the tree, that we might die to sin and live to righteousness. By his wounds you have been healed. (1 Pet. 2:24)

Using nothing more than a simple cross-reference, you can show someone what it means to be "healed" by Jesus's wounds. Christ died ultimately to take care of our biggest problem, our guilt before God on account of our sin. He took on himself the punishment our sins deserved so that we might stand before God with his righteousness, not our own (2 Cor. 5:21).

On the subject of physical healing, you can also ask questions like, "If all believers are supposed to be able to access healing in the atonement, then why does God give the 'gift of healing'?" Or you can read James 5:14 and simply ask, "If all Christians have the ability to claim healing in Jesus's name, then why does the book of James instruct Christians to go to the elders of the church and ask for prayer?"

These questions aren't intended to "win" an argument. But questions like these, asked in a spirit of love and humility, can often plant a seed of doubt that the Spirit may use to lead someone to the true gospel of Jesus.

Consistently Point to the Bible

Scripture is brimming with saints who were loved by God but who nevertheless suffered greatly as part of God's good plan for their lives. Consider some of the people who suffered as children of God. Job was righteous (Job 1:1), yet the Lord willed for him to suffer greatly. But God was glorified in Job's suffering.

Consider the ministry of the apostle Paul. Here was Jesus's promise for Paul's life:

> For I will show him how much he must suffer for the sake of my name. (Acts 9:16)

This was Paul's best life. Listen to Paul describe the fulfillment of God's loving plan:

> Three times I was beaten with rods, once I was stoned, three times I was shipwrecked, a night and a day I have spent in the deep. I have been on frequent journeys, in dangers from rivers, dangers from robbers, dangers from my countrymen, dangers from the Gentiles, dangers in the city, dangers in the wilderness, dangers on the sea, dangers among false brethren; I have been in labor and hardship, through many sleepless nights, in hunger and thirst, often without

food, in cold and exposure. Apart from such external things, there is the daily pressure on me of concern for all the churches. Who is weak without my being weak? Who is led into sin without my intense concern? (2 Cor. 11:25–29 NASB)

Remember, Paul wasn't an enemy of God when he suffered. He was an apostle, chosen by God, and given the grace to be a leader in the early church. He was *called by* God, *faithful to* God, and *blessed for* the glory of God. Yet his life looked like his master Jesus's life: full of suffering.

Which brings us, of course, to the final example of suffering in Scripture: the Lord Jesus himself.

Jesus is the suffering servant of Isaiah (Isaiah 53). He was God's beloved Son (Matt. 3:17). God was well pleased with him (Matt. 3:17). And yet, it was the will of the Father to crush him (Isa. 53:10). Jesus knew this would all happen to him. He knew that suffering was part of the Father's plan for his life (Acts 2:23), and he spoke of it frequently with his disciples (Matt. 16:21).

If Jesus was promised suffering in his service to the Father, then what does that mean for us? No servant is greater than his master (John 15:20). If Christ suffered, so shall we.

> For it has been granted to you that for the sake of Christ you should not only believe in him but also suffer for his sake. (Phil. 1:29)

Sometimes, we think that correcting error or defending the gospel is for "those guys"—pastors, Sunday school teachers, and Christians who just seem to love to argue. But helping those we love to see the error of a false gospel is something that any one of us may be called to do (1 Pet. 3:15). And if the Lord gives us that opportunity, we shouldn't be anxious about it, worrying about whether or not we have the right training or gifts to communicate the gospel (Ex. 4:12; Luke 12:12). If we have open Bibles, humble hearts, love for our neighbors, and the

Spirit of God, then any of us can be used by God to bring light to those in the darkness of the prosperity gospel.

If you've believed in the prosperity gospel, I would ask you to prayerfully consider the verses we've just finished walking through. Ask yourself, does my understanding of the gospel and of the Christian life make sense of the entire testimony of Scripture?[3]

Two Different Gospels

The gospel according to the prosperity gospel is "you can get your best life now." The gospel according to Jesus is "I've forgiven you of your sins. Now take up your cross and follow me" (see Luke 9:23). These are two different gospels.

Do you remember my friend, Roger, from the beginning of the book? To this day, I have a lot of affection for him. He cared for me when few others did.

A few years after I became a Christian, I sat across from Roger and told him that although I loved him very much, I was worried about his soul. By this time, I had come to understand that the prosperity gospel was no gospel at all. I wanted him to know the truth. I wanted to serve him as he had served me. I wanted him to see the beauty of the biblical gospel. I tried to show him that the prosperity gospel was false, and that there was something more, something better. Sadly, Roger wouldn't listen. He rebuked me for my lack of faith, and we parted ways.

As I drove away from Roger's house that day, I was racked with pain and confusion. I wondered what his rejection of the true gospel and his belief in the prosperity gospel meant for his soul.

I'm sure many of you reading this book are wrestling with questions like that. Maybe you're thinking about your friend, your pastor, your parents—and you're trying to untangle a web of spiritual confusion. Perhaps you've come to see for yourself that the prosperity gospel is no gospel at all. What does all this mean?

These questions are weighty, and we don't have time to address them in this booklet. For more help thinking about how to assess the credibility of someone's profession of faith, I would encourage you to read Mike McKinley's book *Am I Really a Christian?*[4]

Ultimately, we need to remember that we are saved only when we place our faith in the true gospel of Jesus Christ. If we place our faith in any other gospel than the one delivered once and for all to the saints (Jude 3), then we are still under the curse of the law (Gal. 1:6–9) and can have no confidence in our salvation.

I remember the first time someone challenged me on the prosperity gospel. I didn't take it very well. If you're in the prosperity gospel and you've made it this far, perhaps God is opening your eyes to a right understanding of the gospel. If so, let me encourage you to find a healthy local church where you can sit under sound expository preaching, be discipled, share your story, begin to heal, and learn to follow Jesus in the fullness of Spirit and truth.

To those readers who may be trying to minister to friends or family still stuck in the prosperity gospel, let me encourage you to not grow weary (Gal. 6:9). Keep praying because our God is sovereign. Keep having challenging conversations. Push your loved ones to think biblically about the gospel, and trust that the Lord will provide understanding (2 Tim. 2:7). And of course, do all this in humility, remembering that it's only by the grace of God that you have come to know the true and beautiful gospel of Jesus Christ (Matt. 16:13–17).

Recommended Resources

Kate Bowler, *Blessed: A History of the American Prosperity Gospel* (Oxford University Press, 2013).

Costi Hinn, *God, Greed, and the (Prosperity) Gospel: How Truth Overwhelms a Life Built on Lies* (Grand Rapids, MI: Zondervan, 2019).

David W. Jones and Russell S. Woodbridge, *Health, Wealth, & Happiness: Has the Prosperity Gospel Overshadowed the Gospel of Christ?* (Grand Rapids, MI: Kregel, 2010).

Notes

1. Personal stories involving other individuals are shared in this booklet with permission. Often pseudonyms have been used for privacy.
2. This story is told more fully in "A Gospel That Almost Killed Me," *9Marks Journal*, Jan–Feb 2014: 13–16, http://www.9marks.org/wp-content/uploads/2014/01/9Marks_Journal_2014_jan-feb.pdf.
3. For two excellent books which explore the biblical gospel see Greg Gilbert, *Who Is Jesus?* (Wheaton, IL: Crossway, 2015); and Gilbert, *What Is the Gospel?* (Wheaton, IL: Crossway, 2010).
4. Mike McKinley, *Am I Really a Christian?* (Wheaton, IL: Crossway, 2011).

Scripture Index

9Marks

Building Healthy Churches

9Marks exists to equip church leaders with a biblical vision and practical resources for displaying God's glory to the nations through healthy churches.

To that end, we want to see churches characterized by these nine marks of health:

1. Expositional Preaching
2. Gospel Doctrine
3. A Biblical Understanding of Conversion and Evangelism
4. Biblical Church Membership
5. Biblical Church Discipline
6. A Biblical Concern for Discipleship and Growth
7. Biblical Church Leadership
8. A Biblical Understanding of the Practice of Prayer
9. A Biblical Understanding and Practice of Missions

Find all our Crossway titles and other resources at 9Marks.org.

John Onwuchekwa

Sam Emadi

Mark Dever

...el Like ...o Church?

Does God Love Everyone?

Matt McCullough

How Can I Find Someone to Disciple Me?

J. Garrett Kell

How Can Women T... the Local...

Keri Folmar

...ized?

How Can Our Church Find a Faithful Pastor?

Mark Dever

Is It Loving to Practice Church Discipline?

Jonathan Leeman

How Can I Love Ch... Members Different...

Jonathan & Andy Ne...

IX 9Marks Church Questions

Providing ordinary Christians with sound and accessible biblical teaching by answering common questions about church life.

For more information, visit crossway.org.